20-5-04.

Animal M

Poems by the
Alderbury and Wes
School

CONTENTS BY THE CHILDREN OF ALDERBURY
AND WEST GRIMSTEAD SCHOOL
Alderbury, Wiltshire, United Kingdom

© The contributors,2004

First published 2004

Published by TheSchoolBook.com
www.theschoolbook.com
t: (+44) 01284 700321

ISBN-84549-001-0

Printed and bound in the United Kingdom

Typeset in Tahoma 11/16

TheSchoolBook.com is an imprint of arima publishing
The IMechE Building, Northgate Avenue
Bury St Edmunds, Suffolk IP32 6BN
www.arimapublishing.com

Contents

CHAPTER 7   127

CHAPTER 1

Owls

Owls' interpretations of the opening lines of Humpty Dumpty

Charlie Scott, Matthew Telfer, Helen Davies, Daniel
Smith, David Wells and Lauren Spreadbury
all agree that
  Humpty Dumpty sat on a wall.

Katie Sell and Harriet Gateley believe
  Humpty Dumpty sat on the wall and then he
  fell off!

However, Bethany Walsh says
  Humpty Dumpty sat on a fish...

Alice Hutchby, Alina Thomas, Frederick Spring,
Alfie Houghton, Aaron Hardy think
  Humpty Dumpty sat on a cat...

Lauren Humphries and Amelia Scadden believe
Humpty Dumpty sat on a bat...

Rebecca King is sure
Humpty Dumpty sat on a cat AND a bat...

George Poulton thinks
Humpty Dumpty sat on a king and a cat...

Kirsty Turner says
Humpty Dumpty sat on a dog...

But Jordan Chant believes
Humpty Dumpty sat on a crocodile!

OUCH!

CHAPTER 2

Badgers

Aaron Lacey

I am Tiny

I can drive a toy boat.
I can speak through keyholes.
I can float on a leaf.

A person looks like a giant.
A twig looks like a log.
A spider looks like an alien.
A computer looks like a cinema.
A leaf looks like a magic carpet.
A pebble looks like a boulder.
A stereo looks like a block of flats.

Alice Heaps

I am Tiny

I can tiptoe into the wind.
I can sneak through trays.
I can creep past a spider.

A little stone looks like a boulder.
The television looks like a cinema.
My teacher looks like a giant.

Badgers Class

Nonsense Poem 1 (with apologies to Spike Milligan!)

On the Bing Bang Bong!
Where the frogs go Bong!
And the children all say Boo!
There's a Bong Bang Bing!
Where the people go Ding!
And the teachers Dibber Dabber Doo.
On the Bong Bing Bang
All the badgers go Bang!
And you just can't catch 'em when they do!

So it's Ning Nang Nong!
Pigs go Bong!
Nong Nang Ning!
Teddies go Jing!
Nong Ning Nang!
The Bees go Bang!
What a noisy place to belong,
Is the Ning Nang Ning Nang Nong!

Badgers Class

Nonsense Poem 2 (with apologies to Spike Milligan!)

On the Fing Fang Fong!
Where the crabs go Bong!
And the teddies all say Boo!
There's a Bong Bang Bing!
Where the people go Ping!
And the children go Tibber Tabber Too.
On the Dong Ding Dang
All the spiders go Bang!
And you just can't catch 'em when they do!

So it's Ning Nang Nong!
Monkeys go Bong!
Nong Nang Ning!
Elephants go Ping!
Nong Ning Nang!
The Clowns go Dang!
What a noisy place to belong,
Is the Ning Nang Ning Nang Nong!

Ben Jones

Dictionary Nonsense

I look in my dictionary
and what do I see?
All the words are muddled up.....
It looks like nonsense to me!

A dinosaur wearing a dress.
A hamster riding a helicopter.
An insect eating an ice-cream.
A ladybird climbing a ladder.
A monkey wearing a mask.
An owl eating an orange.
A penguin eating a pizza.

Oh dear me, what can this be?
Is my dictionary teasing me?

Caitlin Gardner

I am Tiny

I can sneak through windows.
I can creep past a bull-dog.
I can slide on paper.

Grass looks like a zoo.
A puddle looks like a pond.
A car looks like a bus.
A TV looks like a cinema.
A leaf looks like a magic carpet.

Glasses look like mirrors.

Charlie Light

Dictionary Nonsense

I look in my dictionary
and what do I see?
All the words are muddled up.....
It looks like nonsense to me!

A tiger eating a tree.
A sausage riding a scooter.
A pencil poking a policeman.

Oh dear me, what can this be?
Is my dictionary teasing me?

Chelsey Coulbeck

Dictionary Nonsense

I look in my dictionary
and what do I see?
All the words are muddled up.....
It looks like nonsense to me!

A fish cooking food.
A strawberry in a supermarket.
A snail riding a skateboard.
An apple riding in an ambulance.
A pig playing a piano.
A sandal eating a sandwich
A scarf in school
A sausage on a saucer.

Oh dear me, what can this be?
Is my dictionary teasing me?

Chloe Oxford

Dictionary Nonsense

I look in my dictionary
and what do I see?
All the words are muddled up.....
It looks like nonsense to me!

A tiger wearing tights
A penguin eating pizza
A cat in a castle.

Oh dear me, what can this be?
Is my dictionary teasing me?

Conner Houghton

I am Tiny

I can drive a toy bus.
I can fly a paper plane.
I can tiptoe on my sister's
ice cream.

A puddle looks like
the sea. A pebble looks
like a rock.

A leaf looks like
a magic carpet.

Emily Wareham

What Can I See?

I can see it
rainbow rabbit running
in the rain.

I can see a colourful
cat called Caitie
colouring a cake.

I can see sam the squirrel
shaving in the sun.

I can see a guinea-pig growing
grapes in the garden
they are grumpy grapes.

Gemma Fay

I am Tiny

I can sneak through keyholes.
I can tiptoe into cupboards.

A puddle looks like a swimming pool.
A daisy looks like an umbrella.

Jodie Gale

What Can I See?

I can see a clever cat.
I can see a bad badger.
I can see a fat frog.
I can see a red rabbit.
I can see a daft dog.
I can see a funny.
I can see a sad snake.
I can see a pink pig
I can see a happy horse.

Kieran Iles

What Can I See?

I can see a red running rabbity
Rabbit in the rain.

I can see a zapping zibbety
zebra in the zoo.

I can see a bad black and blue biting
banana eating badger in the bathroom.

I can see a clever cross cat
in the clothes.

I can see a silly slithering sausage
snake in the sand.

Lucy Eyres

What Can I See?

I can see a rainbow rabbit
running in the rain.

I can see a colourful cat called
Caitie colouring a cake.

I can see Sam the squirrel
shaving in the sun and
sunbathing on the sand.

Rachel Gray

What Can I See?

I can see a fat frog.
I can see a pink pig.
I can see a funny fish.
I can see a daft dog.
I can see a red cat.

Sarah Bath

Dictionary Nonsense

I look in my dictionary
and what do I see?
All the words are muddled up.....
It looks like nonsense to me!

A scarecrow eating a sausage.
A wizard making some wool.
A chicken eating chips.
A donkey eating a dress.
Gloves on a goat.
An ice cream using an iron.
A ladybird climbing a ladder.
A penguin playing a piano.

Oh dear me, what can this be?
Is my dictionary teasing me?

CHAPTER 3

Hedgehogs

Abigail Townsend

When Winter Comes

When winter comes
people are freezing and sneezing
and have runny noses
and people are teasing.

When winter comes
we eat turkey on Christmas Day
its very fun
and we go out to play.

When winter comes
My mum is cold
We sit by the fire
And the ice is cold to hold.

Adam Telfer

Feet

Feet are for hopping and running
Feet are for walking and skipping
Feet are for jumping and splashing
Feet are for swimming and skating
Feet are for marching and jumping
Feet are for rolling and clinging
Feet are for clinging and sliding

Alex Irving Mayes

I Like...

I like sizzling sausages,
I like marvellous meat,
I like scrumptious sweets,
I like chewy chocolate,
I like better burgers,
I like bitter butter,
I like plum pudding,
I like green grapes.

Alice Scadden

Food I Like

I like sizzling sausages,
I like marvellous meat,
I like sour sweets,
I like jiggly jelly,
I like icy ice cream
I like cream chocolates,
I like bite size biscuits,
I like green grapes,
I like crunchy coconut.

Annabel Salisbury

When Spring Comes

When spring comes
there are fading snowdrops,
fluffy like a pillow
as we spring clean with our mops.

When spring comes
here comes the Easter bunny,
fluffy and white.
It is very sunny.

When spring comes
horses have their foals -
definitely not independent
kicking and making lots of holes.

When spring comes
there are lots of hills
green and flowery
most of them daffodils.

Charlotte Collins

When Winter Comes

When winter comes
there is a big frost.
People can't see very well,
some people get lost.

When winter comes
it is freezing and cold,
soft and smooth
and the ice is cold to hold.

When winter comes
I like to sledge
down the hill
and I fall in the hedge.

Chloe Woodroffe

Painting Children

Flicking fingers flapping.
Messing, mucky, making mess.
Dirty, disgusting, drips, dribbles.
Singing, smiling, squidgy, sneezing.
Colouring carefully, cautiously.

Daniel Cross

Feet

Feet are for running
Feet are for kicking
Feet are for jumping
Feet are for hopping
Feet are for walking
Feet are for sliding
Feet are for dancing
Feet are for skiing

Dennis Turner

Poppy Poem

People dying in the past

Over the sea

Pray for peace

Please wear a poppy

You must never forget

Edward James

Feet

Feet are for standing
Feet are for jumping
Feet are for marching
Feet are for running
Feet are for walking
Feet are for kicking
Feet are for dancing
Feet are for stamping

Ellie Humphries

Poppy Peom

Please wear poppies

Once all the people died in the war

Peace in the world

People dying in the past

You have a minute silence

Emily Caley

When Spring Comes

When spring comes
the Easter bunny comes
fluffy and pudgy
it likes lots of buns

When spring comes
foals run around
white and furry
moles pop up from the ground

When spring comes
flowers bloom
smiling beautifully
they grow in a zoom!!!

Emma Swanston

When Spring Comes

When spring comes
lots of daffodils
grow up and up
there are green hills

When spring comes
out comes the bunny
all pretty and clean hopping round
and its sunny

When spring comes
out comes the blue sky
bluer than anything
and the birds fly by

When the spring comes
there is a bunny
he comes to me and you
hopping all the way and he's funny

Hannah Hutchby

Animal Alphabet

A is for ant
B is for bat
C is for cat
D is for dog
E is for eel
F is for frog
G is for goat
H is for hedgehog
I is for iguana
J is for jaguar
K is for kangaroo
L is for lion
M is for monkey
N is for newt
O is for octopus
P is for polar bear
Q is for quail
R is for rhino
S is for shark
T is for tiger
U is for unicorn
V is for vulture
W is for whale
X is for x-ray fish
Y is for yak
Z is for zebra!

Isabella Gardner

When Winter Comes

When winter comes
when it snows it is freezing
I play outside in the snow
and it starts me off sneezing

When winter comes
I like to sledge
it is fun
but not when I fall in the hedge

When winter comes
I skate on the ice
and it is funny
and it is nice

When winter comes
I eat Christmas turkey
it is very nice
my favourite turkey lurkey

Isabel Noice

School Sounds

Children shouting
Teachers talking
Clocks ticking
Everyone laughing
Kicking a ball
Children stamping

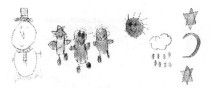

Jack Mullett

Feet

Feet are for running
Feet are for marching
Feet are for dancing
Feet are for walking
Feet are for jumping
Feet are for sliding
Feet are for hopping
feet are for swimming

Harry Palmer

Poppy Poem

Please remember the army

On November the 11th we have two minutes
silence

People dying in the past

Please be peace on earth.

You must always remember us all

Maisie Poulton

Christmas Alphabet

A is for angels up high
B is for bells
C is for crackers
D is for donkey
E is for eve
F if for Father Christmas
G is for Gabriel
H is for holly
I is for ivy
J is for jolly
K is for king
L is for lullaby
M is for Mary
N is for noel
O is for ox
P is for presents
Q is for quiet
R is for red nose
S is for St. Nicholas
T is for tree
U is for under the tree
V is for vicar
W is for wonderful
X is for Xmas
Y is for Yule
Z is for zzz...sleeping

Lottie Trevett

Desert

High, high over the hot, sprinkly sand
Where the slimy rattle snake
wiggles and slithers.
Bumpy camels plodding through
the yellow sand dunes.

Rebecca Ingram

When Spring Comes

When spring comes there are lots of trees
with lots of leaves
and lots of fluttering bees

When spring comes
the sun comes up and it is sunny
the daffodils grow
and you hear people being funny

When spring comes
the cats miaow
and the butterflies flutter by and there are lots of
cows.

When spring comes
all the flowers bloom
and the moles come out of their holes
it all has lots of room

Sophie Smith

Animal Alphabet

A is for ant
B is for bee
C is for cat
D is for dog
E is for eel
F is for fish
G is for goat
H is for hedgehog
I is for iguana
J is for jackdaw
K id for koala
L is for lion
M is for monkey
N is for newt
O is for owl
P is for porcupine
Q is for quail
R is for robin
S is for seal
T is for tortoise
U is for unicorn
V is for vulture
W is for whale
X is for x-ray fish
Y is for yoter
Z is for zebra

Thelma Licence

Schools Sounds

Children shouting
Teachers talking
Clock ticking
Kicking a ball
Chairs scraping
Children crying
Doors creaking
Bell ringing
Paper rustling
Computer buzzing
School Sounds

Tom Froggatt

Poppy Poem

People all over the world

Over the sea

People dying in the past

Peace in the world

You must remember

Tommy Lush

I Like...

I like sizzling sausages
I like marvellous meat
I like strawberry sweets
I like perfect pies
I like green grapes
I like creamy chocolate
I like chocolate cake
I like spicy spagetti
I like mashed mango

Zak Barrett

Christmas Alphabet

A is for angels
B is for bells
C is for crackers
D is for Dasher
E is for eve
F is for food
G is for God
H is for holly
I is for ivy
J is for Jesus
K is for King
L is for lambs
M is for Mary
N is for Nazareth
O is for ox
P is for presents
Q is for quiet...ssshhh
R is for Rudolph
S is for stocking
T is for tree
U is for unwrap
V is for vicar
W is for wise men
X is for Xmas
Y is for Yule
Z is for zzz...

Zoe Blackburn

Desert

High, high over the hot sand dunes,
where the snakes slip their way in the hot sand,
where the palm trees sway in the hot wind
and the caravans walk through the hot sand.

CHAPTER 4

Squirrels

Alexandra Ratcliffe-Russell

The magic tree.

When I am sitting by the tree
I wonder how it feels.
Does he like hearing all
The noise around him?
Does the tree like
Where it stands or does it
Wish it was in the forest
With all the other trees?
Maybe he wishes that he was in a town?
I wish I knew exactly what he feels like.

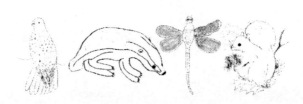

Andrew Bridge

The old pear tree.

The old pear tree
With its pretty golden
Plaque. The only pear tree
In the garden. I couldn't live
Without it with its lovely shade
Keeping me cool in the roasting sun.
It's perfect in every way. Nothing
Wrong with it at all. Some people say
Cut it down but I don't, no way. It's too
Old and beautiful to chop down. I say
It's mine. My mum loves it and so do I.
It would never be the same without me
And my pear tree.

Ben Gray

The magic tree.

I am the magic tree
Tall and old.
In the autumn I am brown and bold.
People sit under me every day,
I give them shade.
People wonder if I like them.
I do.
In the winter people don't sit on me.
I feel like I'm not part of the world any more.

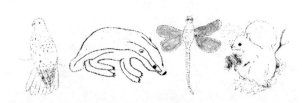

Ben Smigielski

The yew tree.

The yew tree is old.
He is very bold.
He is one thousand years old.
He sometimes glows gold.

Callum Batty

The golden peach tree.

I have a golden peach tree.
It has a swing on the arm of the tree.
It's the only one in the woods.
If it was not there it would not be the same.

Cameron Nelson-Twiby

Colours.

Red like a squashed tomato.
Yellow like a bendy banana.
Green like freshly cut grass.
Blue like a cloudless sky.

Charlotte Iles

Tree in the seasons.

In winter the trees watch the children play
As if they were their own mums.
In spring the trees bloom
As if they were flowers swaying in the grass.
In summer the trees are covered with leaves
Making shade for the children playing in the sun.
In autumn the trees lose their leaves,
They fall to their feet.
Do they like it here?
Do they like it in the world?

Chris Mitchell

The old apple tree.

My tree gives me apples
And I draw it a picture to show it.
My tree gives me apples and gives me shelter.
When it gives me apples it is happy
And smiles at me all the time.

Dominic Sell

The golden beech tree.

There are beech trees everywhere in England.
But my beech tree is the best because it's all gold.
No, really, it's gold and it's the best in the world.
It keeps me cool and I can climb up it when I want
to.
But when I go on holiday I miss my friend.

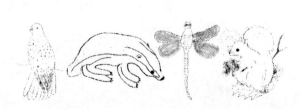

Dylan Smith

My King tree.

My King tree seems real every time it snows.
My King tree hides the snow for me
So I can make snow come.
In autumn his leaves come off
So he doesn't mind me making birds.

Ed Trevett

My Grandpa's tree.

My Grandpa's tree waves in the wind.
My Grandpas' tree seems like it's talking to me
About his days.

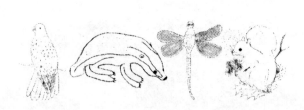

Eloise Sneddon

Leaves.

They fall slowly, delicately down.
They twirl slowly.
They are beautiful colours.

Ewan Walker

The old oak and emperor of all.

My old oak tree stretches over the fence,
The world can see it.
In our garden it's so much like a friend.
Its legs reach through the underworld for miles
and miles.
Its two trunks are legs for the King.
Its beard as long as the world.
Its feet dig and dig through the underworld.
I play I-spy on the neighbours,
Swing on the swing,
Play on the knobs.
It's been there for years.

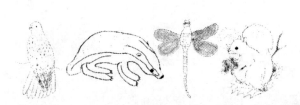

Freya Espir

The happiest apple tree.

When I'm sitting on the swing
On a hot summer's day,
Under my apple tree swing up and down.
When the seconds of wind blow
Into its face
The leaves fall to its feet.
When the rain falls down
The roots fall deeper into the ground.

Gabrielle Hayball

The blossom tree.

Does the blossom tree like the cars going past?
Does the blossom tree like the children leaving him
on his own?
Does the blossom tree like the leaves that have
fallen down?
Does the blossom tree like the children that sit
underneath?

Georgia Thorne

My neighbour's garden.

In my neighbour's garden there is this tree,
And I pick apples from it.
Sometimes I think it looks at me
And I think that it likes me.
I asked it if it liked living here
And one of its leaves fell off.

Jamie Dymond

Drifting leaves.

Slowly drifting down to the ground,
Twirling twirling round and round.
Left to right in slow motion
To the middle of the playground.

Katie Blood

The squirming roots of the empire oak.

The squirming roots slithering to get to the
cleanest soil they can find
While the others find fresh water to store for the
cold winter,
To keep the great fellow warm.
The roots from the ivy help the empire oak to keep
warm
From the wild wet wind from the north.
At night he sings a sweet tune to me that helps me
get to sleep.
I love my oak tree in my garden.

Laura Simpkins

The grand trunk of the magnificent willow.

The break of autumn
Has cracked into life
When the trunk of the grand willow
Stands up high
I think the magnificent hurricane
Will die
Will die
The hurricane will die.

When winter spreads the darkness dreads
Calm is right and
Right is wrong
For a sorrel song
Where the willow was found
Under the whispering of a
Hound.

The grand trunk of the magnificent willow.

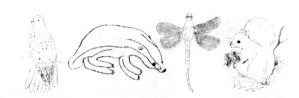

Liam Sharpe

Leaves.

Leaves drifting down
From the magnificent oak tree.
Brown leaves floating
Down onto the floor.

Michelle Cooper

My tall tree.

I like my tall tree rustling.
I like my tall tree giving me breeze.
My tall tree whispers to me at night-time.
When the rain comes down my tall tree gives me
shelter.
I wonder how he feels?

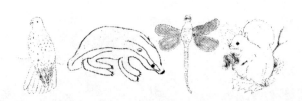

Molly Miller

My big oak tree.

My big oak tree stands elegantly,
Master of all oak trees.
Sometimes I wonder what it feels like
When it's really cold.
In autumn his leaves turn brown.
In winter his leaves are gone.

Oliver Steed

Leaves.

Leaves float down from an oak tree
One by one in the morning.
The trees are bare,
All the lovely leaves are on the floor.

Sam Wareham

My Nan and Grandad's tree.

I feel like my Nan and Grandad's tree is alive,
With its green leaves spreading across the
branches.
When it's ready it drops leaves on the fresh green
grass.
Some leaves land on the summerhouse roof.
To me it's like the tree decides to decorate the
summerhouse roof with green leaves.
But it doesn't bother me.
Under the tree lie some of my best toys
And that feels like the tree wants to play with my
toys too.
My Nan and Grandad's tree also has a secret and
I'm trying to work it out.
I like the shape of the tree too.
May be I'll work out the secret next time.

Scott Quinn

The beech tree.

The beech tree has feelings.
The beech tree can fall when it wants to.
There are beech trees everywhere,
But the one in the woods is my favourite.

Tom Robinson

The magic tree.

The magic tree is old.
People used to play on its old swing
But then it broke.
And the magic tree is of an age
When the magic becomes alive.
The village was as joyful as anything.
The magic tree sways and sways with cold
whispers.

CHAPTER 5

Kingfishers

Adam and Nathan Siviter

New Life

Spring
Lovely fresh smell
Trees begin to bud
Lambs are born
The world is bright and cheerful
Green buds everywhere
New Life

Dominic Fosbraey, Freya Bailey, Sam Jones and Thomas Bayford

Autumn

Wake up in the morning, its very frosty.
As the birds flutter and land
On the branches and sing their songs.
The leaves fall and crumble on the
ground.
Squirrels gather nuts whilst birds fly
south for winter.
Squirrels collect up nuts to eat.
The combine harvester hums as it gathers
The grain slowly but surely.
Fruit falls off the trees and comes
Down with a clump.
Squirrels run along the trees
And all the acorns fall
With the little squirrel chomping at them.

Naomi Hayball, Stephen Press, Shaun Eyres and Jennifer Shone

Autumn

Squirrels getting nuts for the winter time.
The conkers fall from their spiky beds.
The children collect conkers.
Children have conker fights.
Squirrels collect the autumn nuts.
Red leaves falling down.
The autumn leaves fall from the frosty trees
The hedgehogs hibernate in autumn.
Leaves float down like butterflies
And conkers smash against the floor.

Becky Thompson, Sam Bishop, Scott Ingram and Jodie Cullen

All about Autumn

The conkers start to fall
Squirrels are picking hazelnuts
Red breasted robins whistle on the
woody branches
The creamy centred acorns fall to the
dew lit grass
A shimmering conker falls down
through the windy air
All the children run outside into the
autumn garden.

Josie Penfold, Clara Irving-Mayes, Joe Lush and Caleb

Autumn Gifts

Nuts and berries birds and leaves.
Reap the golden harvest wheat.
Leaves change colour die and fall.
Hedgehogs and squirrels hibernate.
The conkers fall and make a tap.
And squirrels gather up the nuts.
And children have conker fights.

Sylvia Palmer, Louis Heaps, Michael Porter and Rebecca Bath

Autumn

The first day of autumn leaves fly smoothly from
the tree.
Squirrels scuttle up the trees.
The moles go back down their holes.
The cobwebs get full,
Of water so the flies don't get caught by the
cobwebs.
Hidden in a tree is a mighty conker.
Covered by a prickly and spiky bright green shell.
Hiding the gleaming conker.
Lots of birds in big crowds
Fly across the sky.
The squirrels scuttling round the ground collecting
nuts.
The leaves fall from the trees and the trees go
bare.
The squirrels gather their nuts and dig them under
the ground.
Playing children run around fields of grassy land,
Gathering blackberries.
Picking and plucking them from bushes.

95

Victoria Gray, Josh Mullett,
Cai Robinson and Alex Allen

Autumn

Blackberries grow on the bushes.
Grapes make wine.
Formers gather the harvest.
Leaves change colour and fall off the
Tree,
Flutter flying to the ground.
The conkers sparkle as they land.
Squirrels run to get their nuts and gather
them up.
The wind blows the fields of grain.

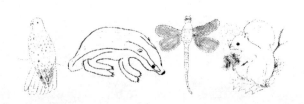

CHAPTER 6

Dragonflies

Amy Vining

Animal Families

My mum is like an octopus because
She's always doing 8 things at
Once.

My little sister is like a
monkey because she's always leaving
mess around so my mum the
octopus has to clean up after her.

My dad is like a tiger because
he's always bringing back food to
eat so my mum has to clean up after
him.

I am like a kangaroo jumping around
all day long.

My brother is like a snail because
he's always leaving a trail around the
house so watch out you might get glowie.

My Grandpa is like an elephant big
and tough.

My Nanny is like a butterfly she's
always wearing different colours.

My cousin is like a mouse she
is as quiet as can be although she
has a little old squeak then goes
back into her house.

My Uncle is like a giraffe
because he is so tall.

My Auntie is like an ant because
she's as small as can be.

Jay Brady

Why Do I Like Cats So Much ?

Why O why do I like cats so much?
Maybe its that they are so cuddly?
Maybe its just me?
Or maybe I was born with it?
so what do you think?

O Why do I like cats so much?
Why couldn't I like dogs?
O well maybe next time I will.

But why do I like cats do you know?
Hmm I should ask a cat
He, she could tell me O why do I like cats so
much?
I should ask my cat or my mum.

I don't know why I like cats so much.
Someone better tell me because I am getting
angry.

So why do I like cats so much.
Do you know?
Please tell me.

The End.

Ben Caley

The Day Before My Birthday

It's the day before my birthday
And I can't wait any more
The suspense is too much to hold
It's like I've been tied down to the floor

I know that I won't
Get to sleep tonight
Thinking about all the things I want to get
Hopefully if I drift off I'll be woken with
delight

With all the things I've wanted
My parents would be broke
But as long as I get something
I'll have a bit of hope!

The day before my Birthday
I absolutely hate
It is so annoying
I really just can't wait!!

Ben Carter

Without a head!

I went to bed with my head on, hoorah!
    And woke up headless, owwer!

I'm going to eat breakfast, hoorah!
    But I don't have a mouth, owwer!

The teachers can't talk 'cos they're headless,
hoorah!
    But so are my friends, owwer!

We're going to play football, hoorah!
    But we can't see the ball, owwer!

I'm going to Top of the Pops, hoorah!
But they're headless too, owwer!

I went to bed with my head on, hoorah!
    And woke up headless, owwer!

Callum Bailey

When I Lost My Head

Last night I woke up with no head.
I was terrified I thought I wouldn't be
able to eat or drink. I was frightened,
I ran screaming to my Mum and Dad
but they didn't hear me. I couldn't hear me
then I thought Oh dear I don't have a
mouth or ears. I went downstairs for food
then I remembered that I don't have a mouth
or teeth so I sliced a piece of battenburg
in to tiny pieces then stuck them in my throat
then I went back to bed and on the cushion I saw
it even though I had no eyes, it was my head
Hallelujah I put it on, I was amazed, I went back
to sleep and was much better in the morning.

Catherine Bayle

The Magic Box

I will put in the box

The roar of the rabbit, the hop of the tiger.
The crackle of the dancing flames
I will put in the box
The bubbles from the parrot and the talking
of the fish.
The caress of the bumble bee.
I will put in the box
the gleaming of the rain-bow.
I will put in the box
The growl of the cat,
The purr of the dog.
I will put in the box
all of my dreams

Cerys Orritt

Without a Soul

I woke up feeling mean like a devil
    my head it was spinning

I was feeling mean I felt good
    My life suddenly felt like never before
       I got up ripped up all my clothes
  except my black top and red jeans
      I felt my head spinning

I ran downstairs ripping all the wallpaper off as I
went
      I ran outside screaming shouting

   I was going to do something mean very nasty

     I was feeling very good really good

I loved the feeling

    I ran somewhere I loved

I came to that place I loved

My heart pounding
running into this garden

I loved it knocking people over as I went

My emotions ran wild

I ran over a bridge
I felt lovely

I jumped into the water I swam to the bottom

Deep

Deep

Deep

Dominic Howieson

The Cat!

the slender body of a cat
that can slip between objects the
silkiness of the fur the
feel of happiness prowling
around the house sensing
any sign of movement with
emerald eyes the cat observes like
a hawk it springs like a
frog to catch its prey its
paws are so soft you'd
wish it cuddled you to
send you asleep zzzzzzzzzzzzz

Edward Atkinson

Animal Families

My mum is like an Owl
Because she is always there when
I need her.
She is also like a Butterfly when
She is calm.

My sister is like a Lion cub
Because she is always exploring
New things although she is scary at the
First offence.

My dad is like a Gorilla
Because he is soft on the
Inside but stubborn on the outside.

I am like a Shark because
I am shy but deadly although I can be like
A Seahorse when I am asleep.

Francis Zieleniewski

A Spring Field

On a sunny spring morning where the trees
are growing buds, a little squirrel comes
out of it's hibernating place and scurried
across the field.

The daffodils are beautiful and bright, a very
shocking yellow, most flowers have now
bloomed completely and the whole field is
outstanding.

Now the children are coming to play,
they are running around getting fit and
making a cold breeze around the field and
making making the squirrel cooler.

Now the children have left to go home so
now the field is peaceful, its getting dark
now but very slowly now the squirrel
falls asleep.

As the night falls upon the field the
owls come out the hooting may
annoy some but not all, so now as
the village sleeps the day ends.

Georgia O'Connor

The Magic Box

I will put in my box
The scent of lovely fresh tulips
The glide of birds swishing by
The roughness of bricks up high in the sky
The softness of foam in a bath

I will put in my box
The brightness of the sky at night
The darkness of the stars
The sound of sweet birds saying
Cock-a-doodle-doo
The sound of a cockerel singing

I will put in my box
Gold and silver satins inside
With fur on the lid
And stars on the lid, secrets
In the corners
With birds feet

Harry Crisp

Crisp Cruncher

The war between man and the crisps.
he rips away the packet the first base down
one man the first sacrifice doesn't give a plenty.
Whole hearted fight, CRUNCH, Crash, he eats him
alive.
They try and hide in the silver foil trenches no
helmets or weapons the war isn't a lot.

Then suddenly a brave cookie breaks and gets
stuck in his throat
he's choking "racha" get me water quick he dies
the war the crisps have won in the gritty trenches
and behind the rubbish sand banks all of them
shout "hooray"
and the tough cookie crisp is now a saint.

Heather Quinn

Animal Families

My mum is like a white rabbit
Because she is hopping mad.

My brother is like a mad and cheeky monkey
Because he drives me bananas.

My dad is like a busy bumble bee
Because he is always busy and works hard.

I am like a noisy hyena
Because I always laugh a lot.

I am also like………..

a buffalo when I am angry because
I charge around
and a zebra when I am bored because
they just stand still
and a koala when I'm tired because
I am slow.

Honey Taylor

The Cat

I own a cat with tiger like stripes,
With aqua eyes that flutter with the wind,
She prowls around the house not wanting
food, but getting some,
At night she pounces on your bed with her
cuddly fur surrounding you,
She enjoys her food and she eats it all, but never
gets fat.
She has a beautiful slender body with the
patterned stripes zig-zagging on her fur,
If she has enough energy she chases mice round
the garden and drags them back into the house,
So I have to clean it all up

MEOW!

Jacob Webb

The Sea

There would be no sea without rivers
There would be no rivers without water
There would be no water without sea
There would be no sea without rivers
There would be no rivers without water
There would be no sea without rivers
There would be no rivers without water
There would be no water without sea
There would be no sea without rivers
There would be no rivers without water
There would be no water without sea
There would be no sea without rivers

Yes, but the question is what
came first water, sea or rivers

The question is unbeknown

James Coveney

The Magical Bike

Once upon a time there lived a boy
called Ben.
And his favourite thing was his golden bike.
He wished that he could do tricks with it.

When he wished really hard
the bike jumped and sparkled.

Suddenly the tricks he wanted to
do, he could do really well.

He entered a bike competition and came
first place.
and then he knew then his bike
was magical

James Whitehead

The Endless Staircase

This is the staircase that never ends.
When you think it's going to end, it won't, because
it never ends, so you will carry on going on and
on and on for the rest of your life. This is the
staircase that never ends. This is the endless
staircase that carries on going on and on and
on……………..
it is never going to end for eternity. The
evil staircase, illuminated by sparkling marble,
glares at you, waiting for you to die.
The haunted, gloomy, evil, endless staircase
that breaks apart and soars away in the
sky.

Joe Bishop

Battlefield

As the misty gun smoke withdraws from it's
dwelling,
it uncovers bodies and you see the winners yelling,
thousands of guns, tanks and men all in a
concentration.
Quickly turns from military might to mass
desolation.
Engines groan and the wounded moan,
and all they want is to return to home.

Amidst the guns firing you hear someone crying
over a soldier who died in battle
doing all he could to prove his metal.

But when people walk there now
They see massive death pits
because they were caused
by guns blowing stuff to bits.

117

Lizzie Oxford

Animal Family

Cat's   purring
dog's   howling
While   lions are prowling.

Bird's   whistling
fish's   swimming
While   foxes are sleeping.

Monkey's swinging
owl's   are hunting
While   bats are sleeping.

Luke Smigielski

A Football Day

At school at playtime we played footy,
It was 2:2 a very tense moment,
It was a lucky kick from a boot,
That scored the winner on the field.

At lunchtime it was between,
The Tornados and the Rhinos,
It was 3:3 and,
The goalie just happened to score the
                    Winner!

And from that day in his school time he
always played in goal.

Max Gill

The Penguin

The penguin waddles along as if it were
on a long trek through a land of arctic antics
searching
searching for a place to swim and hunt.

It opens its wings to balance and so it can waddle
along with its other fellow penguins also in search
for water. They have beaks that shimmer in the
light
so they look like gems from a distance. They've
got
feet like oranges and legs like the smoothest sticks
in the world
painted orange. They have got such fine fur so
when in
water they look like they've got a smooth black
blanket
of velvet wrapped around them.

Naomi Smith

Autumn Fires

Autumn fires's red, orange and yellow
cloud's of smoke towering tall
the crackle of the fire
then the fire growing and
growling the smoke going up and
up and the smoke clashing together
in the sky high high above beyond
the big clouds the smell
of wood burning smoke
towering towering tall
up up up 15ft tall
hours upon hours the flame
is getting smaller and smaller
the flame the flame
has has gone

Nicki Biggs

Friendship

Friendship is like a flowing river
Running freely through the earth
Its like riding on an everlasting friendship horse
Entwining itself between friend and foe
No-one could feel better than they do riding on that
friendship horse
Dancing and jumping over hills and through rivers
Sailing like a ship, open to everyone
Hoping and wishing and flying up high
In that ship is a friendship that
People everywhere hope to find.

Friendship flies high and swishes low
Riding the thermals and plummeting through
streams
Investigating deep into things that no-one knows
about

Entering and exiting people's lives
Nourishing and helping everyone
Discovering things that no-one has ever found
Slipping invisibly into everyone's hearts
High or low, near or far
Inside everyone's hearts is an everlasting friendship that
People hope to find

Friendship is like a flowing river
Running freely through the earth
It's like riding on an
Everlasting friendship horse
No-one could feel happier
Diving deep in friendship
Sailing on a friendship boat
Hoping to weave a wheel of friendship
I own an everlasting friendship that
People hope to find

Thomas Espir

Futuristic Motorbike

The fast slick body of the Davidson
but with no wheels, it goes as fast at
1,000,000 horses and beyond that
Do a jump bounce in to space………. hit a spaceship
and come back down back to earth, bouncing with
no wheels
with a massive engine spluttering and splattering and
SHUT DOWN oooooooo bosh, oops

Tilly Fahie

How Many Things Does it Take

How many thing's does it take to write a
poem you would need the right ingredients
first you need a little mind, the tip of your
finger, a lot of sound and an eye to see
it all, that's how many it does take!!

Tom Walker

MOI E'AD FELL OFF

Moi e'ad fell off
It was eaten by a moth
the moth made a man
and he ate some ham
that was covered in jam
and the jam came from a lamb
the lamb was a sham
the sham was a dam
the dam was a log
the log was a dog
the dog rolled in a bog

CHAPTER 7

Kestrels

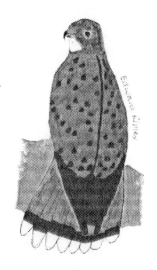

Abby Simmons

Foggy midnight sky

Foggy midnight sky
Coverlet of
Glistening white snow
Naked brittle trees

Ailsa Drew

Frost

Cold
Red nose
Freezing cold toes
Hot bright fire roaring
Wintry

Snow

Blanket
Fluffy snow
Teeth chattering loudly
House shivering in breeze
Freezing

Bethany Witt

Winter

Cosy
Winter's morning
Nothing but silent
Snuggled up in bread
Dreaming

Dreaming

Frosty
Whitened trees
Flakes falling down
Snow dripped holly berries
Silent

Charlotte Hart

Winter

One flower, meekly standing alone
In a battlefield of ice and snow
Slowly weakening against Winter's grasp.
He holds no pity in his cloak of jewelled dewdrops
With his eyes lit up like lanterns, in the darkness
of this world.
His voice is a roaring monster
Echoing through pitch black night,
His breath forming frost in the midnight sky
An icy wind whips frost covered trees
As they shiver in Winter's blind mercy.
But alas, Winter, you have not won
For soon, Summer will surely come.

Charlotte Thorne

Winter

Frost
Teeth chattering
Snowflakes falling silently
White blanket of snow
Frozen

January

Cold
Icicles melting
Hungry birds pecking
Snowflakes falling from the sky
Melted

Christopher James

Snowflake Cinquains

Frost

Teeth
Chattering noisily
Blanket freezing outside
White snow in garden
Winter

Snow

Birds
Very hungry
Icicles dropped
Melted on the ground
gone

Daisy Allen

The Moon

Midnight eyes gazing at a crystal lake
Stars dancing like ballerinas
A face covered in a frost cloak
Carrying a star lighting the night
A town of diamonds, crystals and snow
Black decorated like a Christmas tree
So bright, so beautiful, hypnotism.
A different world, a different life
A tree of ice with blossom of frost
Cries of laughter as the festival begins
Midnight eyes, a gentle smile
Queen of the sky – the moon.

Daniel Telfer

Frost

Icicles
Frozen branches
Snow on rooftops
Beautiful snowflakes still falling
Frost

Winter

Lonely
Freezing Robins
People building snowmen
Inside there's a fire
Freezing

David Huggins

Weather

North winds blew angrily, as houses shivered
As freezing as an iced up lake
The clouds are gloom hanging over
Innocent unsuspecting people
As they continue thier lives normally
January dropped some sleet just now
February will just throw lightning
March will give us rays of hope
Before April comes with sun again
But right now it is bitter
Clouds cover the already dark sky
As we wait patiently for the sun to conquer the
rain

136

Ella Mason

Grandad

Poppies dancing in the wind
Blood lay there like a scarlet carpet
I never knew you Grandad
You died to save our lives
Your blood splashed delicately on the ground
You and others are now below

Emma Cole

Winter Magic

Our wintry magician casts his spell again
As he points his wand
Snowflakes spark out everywhere
Frosty rabbits jump out from under his sparkling
cloak
Another swirl and icicles dangle from sleepy
windows!
Out of his hat fly ghostly doves of frost
Snakes shoot out from his wand
Twisting roads into icy ribbons
As he waves his glittering handkerchief
This powerful magician glides overhead
And drops glittering jewels sparkling in the
moonlight
Children watch in wonder as the snow carries on
through the night

Florence Heaps

Good Night

One winter night I went for a walk
To bid goodnight to my friends
The wind was singing a lullaby
The trees were swaying contentedly
I saw them gradually fall asleep.

Every little snowflake I knew was getting ready
A long day lay ahead
Where children would throw them at each other
Not realising what a shame it was to play with
something so beautiful.
No respect at all, yet my friends enjoy it.
I wonder why?

And every night Lady Moon was always awake
Watching over us constantly
Smiling down at the wide world below.

Good night, I cried, but they never replied ………

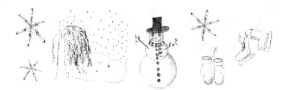

Florence Salisbury

Winter has come

Winter has come
Trees sing in the wind
Like a chorus of angels
But he comes through the snow
Making patterns of ice on window panes.
Freezing what moves.
Birds and rabbits hide away
Terrified to go out.
Nothing at all except snow, ice
And the trees, that are giants
So his work is done.
Jack Frost.

Florence Taylor Jones

The Ice Man

An ice figure with hollow eyes
An eerie chill settles
He walks among a frozen city
No pity in his heart of stone
His eyes of ice stare blankly
Like transparent marbles in their sockets
Even in such coldness
He will not shiver.
He wears a cloak of snow
That almost completely hides
A cruel, ghostly figure.
January is his name.

Gareth Bridge

Winter

Wind has arrived
Whistling roughly and harshly
A roaring fierce lion
Petrifying the frost to the ground
Like a trembling young deer
Frost lands everywhere
As the whistling goes ever on
The icy whiteness piles up in layers
Like an onion growing in the ground
Then snow appears from clouds
Wind calls him howling
As he pushes his snowflakes down to earth.

George Fieldhouse

Poppies of War

Poppies swaying in the breeze
Thin heads bowing in prayer
Remembering all those who died
Poppies flaming red like a carpet of fire
Poppies are so soft like a furry coat
The Poppies are swaying like a river of blood

Kathryn Bacon

Snowflakes

I can't wait for the soft icy snow
To land on my woollen hat and coat
I just can't wait for the whispering snowflakes
Millions of them floating there
But when they land they don't last long
They quiver a while and then die out
Melting into the ground
But as soon as one falls to its death
Another one just as beautiful is found
Only to die minutes later
Each beautiful snowflake seems a waste
I gaze at them, bewildered

Katie Fenlon

White Wonderland

Grey Sky cries tears of ice and snow,
As Sun creeps over Horizon,
Naked Tree's scream is a singing bird,
As is Pansy's in her snowy grave.
But Snowdrop sings a beautiful song,
As sweet as newly made candy,
And Robin joins in as loud as a choir,
So the screams of Tree drown.
World has been wiped clean
Like a canvas, so Spring can come again
To paint its beautiful picture.
Here is Winter.

Katy Bushen

Snowflakes

Freezing
Snowflakes fall
Sometimes they're talking
They are all different
Snowflakes

Frost

Frost
Is here
The patterns printed
On the window pane
Frost

Lorna Noice

Poppies

What is a Flower

A flower as red as a rose
A wave swirling like a soul
People suffering with wind and dirt
People strong and people tough
A breeze blowing your scarlet flowers
What is the flower I am talking about?

Matthew Sell

Creature All Around

Winter is here
Bushes are howling in the wind
As all the animals are hibernating
And all dare not to come out
A Robin and a Wren sing in the breeze
With a high voice
I'm walking and I've seen all this
I am sad to see all these beautiful things
disappear
The wind was like a roaring fire
I was scared as a mouse seeing a Lion
So Winter is here at last
Let's all go and have a snowball fight

Maxine Sharpe

Winter

Freezing
Snowflakes falling
From wintry sky
My garden covered in
Snow

Molly Newman

Sunny Spain

White Villa's shining in a warm sun
Palm trees swaying and coconuts falling
Smell drifting of freshly baked bread
Having lunch with beautiful views
Beaches packed, no where to sit
People laughing and having fun in a big bright sun

Peter Saunders

The Sadness of War

The nodding heads of the Poppies in the breeze
The whispering of war tales from bowing poppies
The battle field with patches of blood
Brave men and women who gave their lives
A wave of red in the fields
The sadness in the battle fields

Rachael Thompson

Poppies

Poppies are scarlet reds
Swaying in the breeze
Like a sea of blood
Waving at me as they splash in the sunlight
Poppies are delicate like the wounded soldiers
Poppies are for remembrance

Richard Fry

Winter Battle

As a ferocious wind strolled in on its steed
Trees start to talk about winter's ferocious battles
Animals scamper into the distance
As winter gale, frost and snow to the land
And a village prepare for a ferocious battle
Then suddenly spring appears out of nowhere
On its' dazzling steed of green flames
It was bright no one could gaze upon its beauty
Except for cold hearted winter
As winter drew its blade so did autumn
Then a battle broke out as autumn started to loose
Winter fell down a hole as January strolled in

Sophie O'Connor

Ice Figures

As the New Year arrives
January is getting ready for war
Making icy armour and snowy helmets
Ice figures carved in the street
Standing staring in the distance
Paying no attention
January is a gentle snowflake
Ready for war now
Ice figures like soldiers waiting for signals
Signals are given now
Ice figures running to battle

Edward Ripley

The battle

As frost taken lands appear,
Jack frost is freezing lands of good,
 As January mounts his lighting steed,
And rides forth quicker than light,
To war he goes like an eagle catching prey,
January is coming like an eerie ghost,
Swooping over shadowy trees ,they seem to say
good luck,
As January takes back his taken lands,
He strides up proudly to jack frost himself,
Jack frost takes a swoop of his icy cat like claws,
January takes out his mighty axe,
And flings it, and cuts down his foe.

Thomas Vining

Ice

Icicles
Hanging above
A white door
Putting grit on roads
Ice

Freezing

Frost
Teeth chattering
Snowflakes falling silently
A drifting blizzard sky
Snowflakes

Tim Moulsdale

Winter

Trees stand proudly like soldiers
Wind whistling, like a child screaming
Fire is swirling, burning with laughter
Snowflakes drift to earth they live then die
Frost on the window as beautiful as snow
An icy pond, like millions of crystals
Christmas rose with a blanket of snow
The grass sparkles as though it's been covered in
diamonds
A Robin is perching on a branch quiet and still
Whispering snowflakes
The moon is high silvering the trees
Winter

Timmy Shallcross

Freezing

Freezing
Just freezing
So so freezing
Just absolutely stupidly freezing

Cat

Where
Is Mittens
I see lumps
Of snow but no
Mittens

Tom Good

Winter

Winter is here, as white as a dove.
Snowdrops are alive, Christmas roses are too,
Rabbits hibernating in a burrow,
Cars are now going to sleep, refusing to move.
Winter and January have teamed up
To cause isolation to block the summer's grasp.
The wind is angry, making ghastly noises,
Making awful gusts nearly pushing over trees.
Jack Frost is about, nibbling children's toes,
Making frost block up windows.
Winter is here, snow is falling.
So let's go out and have a snowball fight!

William Froggatt

Poppies of Life

Lanes of Poppies standing in fields
Reminding people of war and of life
A carpet of red and colour swaying breeze
Poppies being torn from the ground
Like men being ripped from their bodies
People falling asleep but never to wake
Poppies of life

Zoe Cullen

Snowy

Dripping
Icy snow
A white garden
Soft snow falling snowflakes
Shivering

Birds

Shivering
Freezing cold
Catching happy birds
Asking for some food
Frosty

Printed in the United Kingdom
by Lightning Source UK Ltd.
100680UKS00001B/148-198